"An awesome book specifically tailored for children ages eight to twelve. Through relatable stories, this workbook offers simple, practical activities that will help kids navigate their worry, sadness, anger, and other intense emotions. Whether used independently or alongside a parent or therapist, the exercises are a transformative tool to empower kids to deal with their thoughts and feelings with greater awareness, effectiveness, and self-kindness. Brava to Tamar for providing a gift that promises to contribute throughout the course of the developmental period and beyond."

> —**Steven C. Hayes, PhD**, co-originator of acceptance and commitment therapy (ACT)

"*The ACT Workbook for Kids* is the fun, engaging, and helpful workbook I've been waiting for in my practice and in my own family!"

> —**Christopher Willard, PsyD**, faculty at Harvard Medical School, and author of *Growing Up Mindful*

"Just what clinicians who work with children need: a beautifully designed, practical, easy, and delightful romp through kid-sized ACT skills. I suspect that the activities in this workbook will be so much fun that kids will barely notice they are learning substantial skills to help them navigate life's storms and challenges mindfully—with openness to learn from their emotions, and trust in their ability to do hard things that they care about."

> —**Lisa W. Coyne, PhD**, faculty at Harvard Medical School, and coauthor of *Stuff That's Loud* and *Stop Avoiding Stuff*

"This delightful workbook is filled with activities that support counseling sessions with kids. The reader will find fun, engaging, and easy-to-use experiences. Kids can practice expressing their feelings and thoughts while learning to be aware of ineffective and effective responses. If you're a busy professional, you'll find the worksheets perfect to integrate into your work."

> —**Louise L. Hayes, PhD**, clinical psychologist; founder of DNA-V; and author of *Get Out of Your Mind and Into Your Life for Teens*; *Your Life, Your Way*; and *The Thriving Adolescent*

"What a lovely book! *The ACT Workbook for Kids* is not only beautifully constructed and illustrated, but also an inviting and approachable learning experience for kids. It is a wonderful journey from front to back where children can discover and open up to their emotions, and work on what is important to them. A wonderful dash of learning self-compassion is also part of this must-have book for kids!"

> —**Robyn D. Walser, PhD**, licensed clinical psychologist; author of *The Heart of ACT*; and coauthor of several books, including *Learning ACT* and *The ACT Workbook for Anger*

"The ACT Workbook for Kids is an amazing book that is fun and engaging. It is a must-have book for children and therapists."

—**Ben Sedley**, clinical psychologist, and author of *Stuff That Sucks*

"There's no getting around it—working with strong feelings and thoughts is hard! In this wonderful book, Tamar Black translates the core processes of ACT into a delightful buffet of activities that are deep, helpful, and—dare I say it—fun. This isn't a book you read, it's a book you do. And it's a book that will benefit all children who encounter it. Highly recommended!"

—**Russell Kolts**, PhD, author of *CFT Made Simple, An Open-Hearted Life*, and *Experiencing Compassion-Focused Therapy from the Inside Out*

"This book is an absolute gem. It has made me realize just how much I needed it when I was a child. Heartwarming, easy to read, and incredibly helpful—it caters to kids, therapists, teachers, parent figures, and anyone seeking to connect with their inner child. Get ready to embark on a transformative journey with the assurance that you are in exceptionally capable hands."

—**Rikke Kjelgaard**, psychologist, author, and ACT trainer

"A helpful tool for youth ages eight to twelve, and their parents. The workbook uses story examples to show kids how to address difficult thoughts, feelings, and bodily sensations. Readers are guided through mindfulness, support building, self-compassion, and values identification as they discover they are more than their experience. This is a must-have book for prevention and intervention!"

—**Amy R. Murrell**, PhD, coauthor of *The Joy of Parenting; To Be With Me;* and *The Becca Epps Series on Bending Your Thoughts, Feelings, and Behaviors*

"This book is an absolute treasure chest, full of fun and engaging exercises to help kids learn from and understand even the most challenging experiences. Like an interactive game, this book is creative, powerful, and fun."

—**Janina Scarlet**, PhD, award-winning author of *Superhero Therapy*

"An invaluable workbook that offers engaging activities and relatable scenarios to help children better understand and manage their emotions. This essential resource for parents, educators, and therapists provides gentle and creative guidance, encouraging kids to become more resilient and self-aware. A highly recommended tool for children ages eight to twelve, and their caregivers."

—**Mavis Tsai**, PhD, cocreator of functional analytic psychotherapy; and founder of the Awareness, Courage & Love Global Project

The ACT Workbook for Kids

Fun Activities to Help You Deal with Worry, Sadness & Anger Using Acceptance & Commitment Therapy

Tamar D. Black, PhD

Instant Help Books
An Imprint of New Harbinger Publications, Inc.

Publisher's Note

INSTANT HELP, the Clock Logo, and NEW HARBINGER are trademarks of New Harbinger Publications, Inc.

New Harbinger Publications is an employee-owned company.

Copyright © 2024 by Tamar D. Black

Instant Help Books
An imprint of New Harbinger Publications, Inc.
5720 Shattuck Avenue
Oakland, CA 94609
www.newharbinger.com

All Rights Reserved

Cover design and illustrations by Sara Christian

Interior book design by Amy Shoup

Acquired by Tesilya Hanauer

Edited by Elizabeth Dougherty

Printed in the United States of America

26   25   24

10   9   8   7   6   5   4   3   2   1   First Printing

This book is dedicated
to the children and parents
I work with—past, present,
and future. Thank you
for allowing me to be a
part of your journey.

Contents

Section 3: Choose What Matters and Do What Matters

Section 4: Stay Here and Notice Yourself

Section 5: Be Kind and Caring to Yourself

Section 6: Putting It All Together

Foreword

I was so excited when I found out that Tamar was writing this book. I'd been hoping she would. In 2022, Tamar wrote an excellent textbook for counselors and therapists called *ACT for Treating Children*. This new workbook for kids makes a fantastic companion piece.

And, boy, do we need it. Because, the sad truth is, while society places huge importance on teaching kids to read, write, and do math, there's *way* less emphasis on equally important life skills, such as how to handle painful thoughts and feelings and do difficult things you really care about.

That's where this book comes in. Although it's based on acceptance and commitment therapy (ACT), it's a book that's useful for any child—not just those who, for one reason or another, see a therapist. Why do I say this? Because *all children suffer.* Every child encounters failure, disappointment, and rejection. Every child experiences difficult emotions, like sadness, anger, and anxiety. And every child has self-judgmental thoughts about not being good enough.

The sooner kids learn how to effectively handle these inevitable, painful aspects of life, the better. This book helps make that possible. The activities in these chapters are simple, powerful, engaging, playful, and practical. Kids can do them by themselves—or with the help of a parent or therapist. As kids work through this book, they will develop a truly life-enhancing skillset.

They'll learn how to cope with difficulties, face fears, rise to challenges, recover from setbacks and disappointments, treat themselves compassionately, discover what is truly important to them, do things that truly matter to them—and effectively handle all those difficult thoughts and feelings that life dishes up for all of us.

Whether the child in question is one of your own offspring or a client you work with, rest assured, they are in good hands. Enjoy the journey.

—RUSS HARRIS
Author of *The Happiness Trap*

Acknowledgments

I wish to acknowledge the Boonwurrung people of the Kulin Nation as the Traditional Owners and Custodians of the land on which I reside, work, and wrote this book. I pay my respects to their Elders past, present, and emerging, and acknowledge and uphold their continuing relationship to this land.

To the team at New Harbinger Publications, thank you so much, especially Tesilya Hanauer—for inviting me to write this book and for your enthusiasm, guidance, support, and assistance—and Caleb Beckwith. To freelance editor Elizabeth Dougherty, thank you so much for all of your assistance.

To my best friend and husband, Gavin, thank you for your love, encouragement, and unlimited support. To my children, Sara and Ariella, thank you for always cheering for me. To my parents, Ruth and David, thank you for your unconditional love, encouragement, and support of my dreams.

A Letter to Parents and Professionals

Hi, I'm Tamar Black, an educational and developmental psychologist in Australia, with more than twenty years' experience working as a school psychologist and in private practice. I work with children, teenagers, and parents. I have expertise in acceptance and commitment therapy (ACT), which is a form of cognitive behavioral therapy (CBT). I also wrote the book *ACT for Treating Children* for therapists working with kids five to twelve years of age. This workbook is for kids eight to twelve years of age to help them with worry, sadness, anger, and other strong thoughts and feelings. Doing the activities with a parent or therapist can also benefit younger children who are struggling with difficult emotions. You'll meet three fictitious kids—Maria, Aiyden, and Jia—and follow them on their journey, learning how they used ACT to help themselves.

Kids don't have to do every activity in this book—you might help them select some, or they might decide on their own. Depending on their age, you might need to help them spell or write, and there are some craft activities they might need your help with. I don't recommend reading the whole book at once—perhaps try two or three activities each week. The more kids practice the techniques in their day-to-day life, the more they will use what they have learned to deal with their thoughts and feelings.

If you are a therapist, you don't need any prior training in or knowledge of ACT in order to use this book with your clients. I recommend also reading my other book, *ACT for Treating Children*, and using this book as a companion. You can use the activities in this book in therapy sessions with kids and select some as home tasks for them to do on their own or under a parent's supervision.

Thanks so much for reading,

Tamar

A Letter to Kids

Hi! My name is Tamar. I'm a child psychologist. I talk to people and try to help them deal with their thoughts and feelings. Some kids I work with call me a "talking doctor." I've worked at a school and in a clinic for more than twenty years. I also help parents help their kids with their feelings.

I wrote this workbook for kids eight to twelve years old to help them deal with strong feelings, like worry, sadness, and anger. You can read this book on your own. Or you can read it with a parent or another adult. I'll teach you activities you can do to help yourself. You can try them even if you aren't having any difficult feelings right now. In this book, you'll meet Maria, Aiyden, and Jia. They are three kids who learn how to deal with their thoughts and feelings.

The activities will teach you different ways to deal with thoughts and feelings. These will help you to help yourself when you feel worried, sad, angry, and other feelings. Try to do activities two or three times a week. The more you practice, the better you will become at using what you learn when you need help dealing with your thoughts and feelings.

Thanks so much for reading,

Tamar

Dealing with Your Thoughts and Feelings

Your mind is often very busy doing lots of thinking. Your mind also has lots of feelings. Sometimes your thoughts and feelings are very strong. In this book, you'll learn ways to deal with your thoughts and feelings. But first I want to introduce you to three kids.

INTRODUCING MARIA, AIYDEN, AND JIA

Maria, Aiyden, and Jia had a hard time dealing with their thoughts and feelings. Then they learned new ways to deal with strong feelings like being worried, sad, or angry. They use these actions at home, school, and other places, like the mall, parties, sports events, and friends' houses.

Now, let's meet Maria, Aiyden, and Jia.

MARIA, *Twelve Years Old*

Maria had lots of worries. Often her mind told her that something bad would happen. Her mind had *lots* of power over her, because she believed everything it said. Maria worried about going to places like school, friends' homes, the doctor's office, and the mall. She also worried about going on trips with her family. Maria didn't want to leave her home when she worried. Her parents wanted to take her and her brothers to interesting places, but Maria didn't want to go because she worried so much. Maria felt sad about missing out on school and on having fun with her friends. She wished she could go to school and other places too.

AIYDEN, *Ten Years Old*

Aiyden often felt annoyed and angry when his parent asked him to help out. He felt the same way when a teacher asked to see his homework or kids at school didn't do what he wanted. When Aiyden felt annoyed and angry, his body felt really hot, and his stomach felt tight. He would also shout and cry. Sometimes he kicked a wall or slammed a door. At home, he argued a lot. His sisters didn't want to play with him because they were scared of him. At school, kids didn't want to play with him either. They worried that Aiyden would shout if he didn't win games. Aiyden also became upset and angry when places were noisy. He wanted the classroom and his home to be very quiet. He thought that no one understood his thoughts and feelings. Aiyden also felt very lonely.

JIA, *Eight Years Old*

Jia's family got a dog for her fourth birthday. She named him Scout. Jia loved Scout very much. She liked brushing him, helping bathe and feed him, and taking him to the park. Scout got sick, and one day he died. Jia was very sad and missed Scout a lot. She worried that when she was at school or at friends' homes, she would think about Scout and cry. She tried very hard to forget about Scout. But no matter how hard Jia tried, she kept thinking about Scout. She didn't know what to do with her thoughts and feelings. It was hard for Jia to enjoy playing with her friends and going to their homes because her mind kept thinking about Scout.

ACTIVITY 1

Feelings You Would Like Help With

Look at the feelings below and on the next page and think about which ones you would like some help with. These feelings might show up when you feel worried, sad, or angry. You can write the names of other feelings you would like help with in the empty shapes. **Circle the feelings you picked or color in their shapes.**

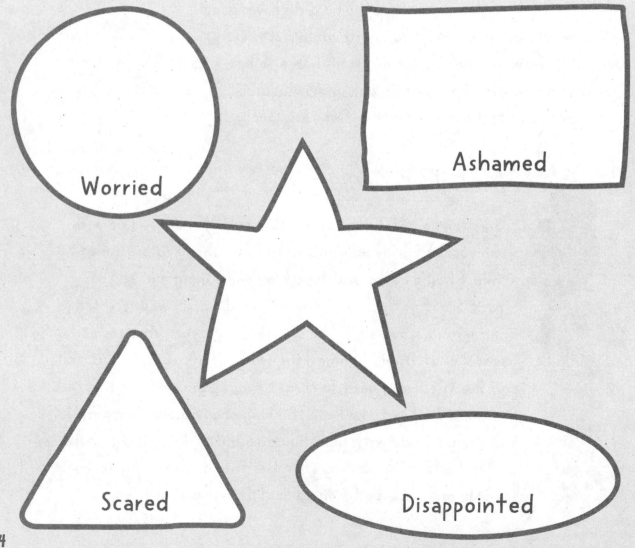

Worried

Ashamed

Scared

Disappointed

Annoyed

Nervous

Sad

Jealous

Guilty

Angry

5

"How Much You Care" Ruler

Sometimes your feelings are really strong. When you feel very worried, sad, or angry, it's helpful to ask yourself how much you care about what you are worried, sad, or angry about. Thinking about how much you care about something can help you understand and describe your feelings. It can also help you choose whether to react or not. But you can also choose not to react, or to only react a little, even when your feelings are strong.

This activity uses a ruler to help you measure how much you care about something. This can help you decide whether it's worth getting worried, sad, or angry about. It can also help you calm yourself. For example, you've been looking forward to bike riding today, but discover that your bike has a flat tire. The bike stores are closed. You feel very angry and want to scream. You calm yourself by telling yourself that because you care about bike riding, you are disappointed that you can't ride. You hope that your parent will be able to get the tire fixed soon.

The rulers below are numbered from 0 to 10.

- Number 0 is something you care about but not much. For example: It's warm today.

- Number 10 is something you care the most about. You would be very worried, sad, or angry if it happened. For example: You are really excited to go on a ski trip, but you break your leg the day before and can't go.

0 1 2 3 4 5 6 7 8 9 10

Use the numbers to measure how worried, sad, or angry you feel. As the numbers get bigger, the hearts get bigger too. The hearts show how much you care. The bigger the heart is, the more you care and feel that feeling.

WORRIED

- Imagine something happening that you would feel very worried about. **Write what it is next to number 10.**

- Think about something that you would not worry about at all. **Write what it is next to number 0.**

0 1 2 3 4 5 6 7 8 9 10

_____   _____

SAD

- Imagine something happening that you would feel very sad about. Write what it is next to number 10.

- Think about something that you would not care about at all. Write what it is next to number 0.

0   1   2   3   4   5   6   7   8   9   10

_____   _____

ANGRY

- Imagine something happening that you would feel very angry about. Write what it is next to number 10.

- Think about something that you would not feel angry about at all. Write what it is next to number 0.

0   1   2   3   4   5   6   7   8   9   10

_____   _____

ACTIVITY 3

When Do Your Thoughts and Feelings Show Up?

Knowing when your thoughts and feelings show up can help you be ready for how you might feel. Then you'll know what to do to help yourself. In this activity, you're going to think about examples of things that make you feel worried, angry, or sad. Then you'll write down more details. I have written an example for you.

- In the "What Happens" column of the table below, write down things that happen that make you feel worried, sad, or angry.

- Fill in the next three columns by writing down where this happens, what your mind thinks, and how you feel.

- Look back at the "how much you care" ruler in Activity 2 and the things you rated a 10. These are things that you care a lot about. They would make you feel very worried, sad, or angry if they happened. In the last column of the table, write down a number from 0 to 10. Pick a number that shows how much you care about what happens compared to those things that would upset you a lot.

WHAT HAPPENS	WHERE THIS HAPPENS	WHAT MY MIND THINKS	HOW I FEEL	NUMBER ON "HOW MUCH YOU CARE" RULER
My favorite show isn't on TV tonight.	At home	I want to kick the TV.	Angry	4

Your Body Map

When you feel worried, you might feel tight in your stomach. When you feel sad, you might cry. When you feel angry, your face, ears, neck, and the rest of your body might feel hot, like your skin is burning. Different people's bodies react in different ways to different feelings.

Let's do an activity to help you find out where your feelings show up in your body.

HOW TO MAKE THE BODY MAP

Before you start, ask your parent if you can have a photo of yourself to cut up and stick on this page, or if they can print a photo of you. The photo should show your whole body. If you don't have a photo, you can draw a picture of yourself.

MATERIALS

- Photo of yourself that shows your whole body

- Glue or tape

- Colored marker, pen, or pencil

INSTRUCTIONS

- Cut off any background in the photo, so that what remains is only your body in the photo. You may need to ask a parent for help cutting the photo.

- Glue or tape the photo in the image of the picture frame.

- Think about where in your body you feel worried, sad, or angry. Write the feeling next to that part of your body.

- What could you do to calm these parts of your body when you feel worried, sad, or angry? Write this next to the feelings.

- When you feel worried, sad, or angry, look at this body map as a reminder of where your feelings show up and what to do to calm these parts of your body.

13

What Do Your Feelings Look Like?

Think about your strongest feeling of being worried, sad, or angry. Now imagine what that feeling might look like if you could see it. Is it big or small? What color is it? What name could you give that feeling?

When you feel worried, sad, or angry, imagine that you see the feeling. Then give it a name. This will help you understand how you feel. The feeling might not feel as strong anymore.

Draw or paint that feeling on the next page. Then write a name for that feeling above it.

Let It Be and Let It Go

Sometimes things turn out differently from how you thought they would. Can you think of a time like this? Maybe in the morning the sun was shining, and the sky was blue. You planned to play sports at lunch at school. But right before lunch, the sky filled up with big, dark clouds. It rained all through lunch, so you had to stay inside.

We don't always know how things are going to be, and that's okay.

Now you'll learn how you can use *let it be* and *let it go* to deal with your thoughts and feelings. When you let your thoughts and feelings be, and then let them go, they aren't as powerful. This can help you become more powerful.

LET IT BE

Let it be means not doing anything with your thoughts and feelings. You don't try to get rid of them or think about something else. Instead, your thoughts and feelings can be there. Let it be is often a great place to start trying to deal with your thoughts and feelings.

Aiyden Lets It Be

Aiyden worried about places being noisy and tried very hard not to think about this. But the more he tried, the more his mind worried. Aiyden tried to think about other things instead, like what was for dinner or playing with his pet guinea pig. But his worries about noise didn't go away. Aiyden felt *really* angry. He also felt annoyed.

Then Aiyden learned to let his thoughts be. He let his mind think whatever it wanted to, even about noise. He practiced letting his thoughts and feelings be every day. This means that he stopped trying to tell his mind not to think about things. He even told his mind it could think about whatever it wanted to. Aiyden stopped trying to get rid of his thoughts. When he let his thoughts be, Aiyden was okay. His thoughts didn't hurt him.

 **TIP**

Trying to get rid of your thoughts and feelings gives them more power. Instead, try to let your thoughts and feelings be when you're at home, school, or somewhere else.

LET IT GO

When your thoughts feel really strong, they can feel like they're stuck to you. When you *let it go*, you see your thoughts as just thoughts that aren't always true. You don't have to believe all the thoughts your mind tells you. This helps make your thoughts less powerful. Letting it go can help you move on quickly when you feel worried, sad, angry, or other strong feelings. It can also help you have fewer fights.

Maria Lets It Go

Maria's family wants to go to the park next week for a picnic, but Maria is afraid of storms and worries that it will rain. She worries about getting wet and cold. The more she tried not to think about rain and storms, the more worried and scared she became. Maria was sad. She didn't want to miss out on the picnic.

Then Maria learned to let her thoughts go. She stopped believing everything her mind told her. Her thoughts felt less powerful. She was able to go to the picnic, and when her mind worried about rain and storms, she said to herself I'm having the thought that it might rain. This helped Maria enjoy the picnic. It also helped her do things like go to school, go to friends' houses, and go to the mall, even when her mind worried.

 TIP

When you have a thought, try saying, "I'm having the thought that..." followed by the thought. For example, if you think that you are worried, try saying, "I am having the thought that I'm worried." Or you could say, "My mind is telling me that I'm worried."

Don't Think About "Ice Cream"

The following activity is like an experiment in whether you can tell your mind not to think about something. I'd like to invite you to try to not think about ice cream.

Look at the picture of the ice cream cone. Let your mind think about whatever it wants to. But don't think about ice cream! Don't think about how your favorite ice cream tastes, what it feels like on your tongue, or if you like it in a cone or cup.

How did that go? What did you think of? Were you able to not think about ice cream? I wasn't able to. My mind kept thinking about ice cream melting and dripping down a cone. **Was it easy to not think about ice cream or difficult?**

_____

_____

_____

_____

_____

_____

Leaving Your Thoughts Alone

Let's do an activity to help you pick out a few thoughts you'd like to try and let be.

- In the first column of the table on the next page, write down a few thoughts you try to tell your mind *not* to think about.

- In the next column, for each thought, write down whether this is easy or hard to do.

- Choose one or two thoughts that you'd like to practice letting be. Highlight these thoughts with a light color marker or circle them.

- During the week, try to practice letting these thoughts be.

You can come back to this activity to remind yourself of the thoughts you are going to try to let be.

WHAT THOUGHTS DO YOU TRY TO TELL YOUR MIND *NOT* TO THINK ABOUT?	IS THIS EASY OR HARD TO DO?

Inviting Your Thoughts and Feelings

When you feel worried, sad, angry, or some other strong emotion, sometimes your mind tells you that you should stay home or stay in your bedroom until you feel better. When you believe everything that your mind tells you, you give your mind lots of power.

Instead of trying to get rid of your thoughts and feelings, try inviting them to join you. You might like to pretend that your thoughts and feelings can hold your hand, walk next to you, or ride with you. This helps you to be more powerful. Here's what happened to Jia when she asked her sad feelings to join her.

Jia's Story

When I woke up in the morning and remembered that my dog Scout had died, I felt sad. I wished he were still running around and wagging his tail. I tried hard not to think about Scout. My mom told me to think of happy things, but that didn't work. The more I tried to forget about Scout, the sadder I felt! I learned that I didn't have to get rid of the sad feeling. Instead, I could ask sad to join me. I stopped trying to forget about Scout. When it was time to go to school, I said, "Come on, sadness, it's time to go to school now." At school, I was okay when my mind thought about Scout and told me I was feeling sad. I could keep doing my work.

What does your mind tell you to do when you feel worried, sad, angry, or some other strong feeling? **Write your answers below.**

_____

_____

_____

_____

_____

_____

_____

_____

_____

_____

Create an invitation to your thoughts and feelings, inviting them to join you. Decorate the invitation by coloring it in or putting stickers on it.

You're Invited

ACTIVITY 9

Choosing Helpful Actions

Sometimes you do things when you feel sad that don't help. When you feel sad, spending a long time alone can make you feel worse. Sometimes spending time with other people or doing things you care about can help make you feel better.

Let's look at some of the actions Jia did when she felt sad. Some things helped Jia feel better. Others made her feel even sadder.

Circle the actions below that you think helped Jia. (The answers are on the next page. But don't look at them until after you have finished this activity.)

I'm staying in my bedroom until I stop feeling sad.

I miss Scout today, but I'm still going to school.

I sat by myself at lunch at school because I felt too sad to sit with my friends.

I told my parent how I was feeling.

When I thought about Scout, I did a drawing.

I tore all the photos of Scout into little pieces.

I spoke to my teacher about how much I miss Scout.

I didn't go to my friend's house because I was sad.

What do you do most often when you feel sad?

_____

_____

_____

_____

_____

Is this a good thing to do? Or does it make things worse?

_____

_____

_____

_____

_____

These are the actions that help Jia feel better:

I miss Scout today, but I'm still going to school.

I told my parent how I was feeling.

When I thought about Scout, I did a drawing.

I spoke to my teacher about how much I miss Scout.

27

Saying Hello to Your Thoughts and Feelings

A great way to let your thoughts and feelings be is to make friends with them and say hello to them. This helps you see your thoughts as just words. Then they are less powerful. You do not have to let your thoughts boss you around. You could say:

- *"Hello, worries, it's great to see you again!"*

- *"Hello, scared, how are you?"*

- *"Welcome back, sadness. I love how you've done your hair!"*

Write down some ways you could say hello to the thoughts and feelings that are listed in the following table. This will help you to remember how to let your thoughts and feelings be. Some examples are provided. Fill in the blank spaces.

THOUGHT	WAYS TO SAY HELLO
I'm not going to do well in my test.	Hello, I'm not going to do well in my test.
I don't know who to play with at school.	Hello, I don't know who to play with at school. I love your T-shirt!
I'm very sad.	Hello, sadness. It's good to see you again.
I'm so scared.	
I feel like crying.	
You are making me so angry.	
I'm very angry this happened.	

HOW MARIA SAID HELLO TO HER WORRIES

Let's look now at what Maria did that helped her when she felt worried.

Maria was practicing playing piano for her recital, but her mind told her she was worried. Maria said, "Hello, worries, it's lovely to see you again. I've missed you!" Then she giggled. She practiced playing piano, even when her mind said she might make mistakes. When Maria's mind worried about playing piano in front of all the parents at the recital, she said, "Hello, worries, my friend, what have you been doing?" Saying hello to her worries helped Maria and made her mind less powerful. This also helped Maria worry less.

ACTIVITY
11

Making a Glitter Bottle

Another way to help let your thoughts be is with a glitter bottle.

HOW TO MAKE A GLITTER BOTTLE

Let's take a look at how you can make a glitter bottle and use it to let your thoughts be.

MATERIALS

- Small plastic bottle with a lid

- Food coloring dye (light color)

- Dishwashing liquid

- Coarse glitter or glitter shapes in a few different colors (if the glitter is too fine, it won't sink to the bottom)

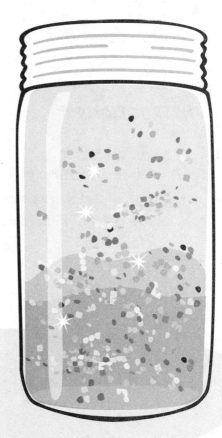

INSTRUCTIONS

- Fill the bottle with water and add just one drop of food coloring dye. If the food coloring dye is too dark, you won't be able to see the glitter. If it's too dark, empty out most of the water and add plain water to fill it up again.

- Add a drop of dishwashing liquid. This helps the glitter float.

- Add the glitter.

- Tightly close the bottle lid.

HOW TO USE A GLITTER BOTTLE

The glitter is like your thoughts. The bottle is like your mind. **Pick up the bottle and turn it up and down a few times. Watch what happens.** When you shake up the bottle, the glitter moves around. Do you sometimes feel like you've got a lot of thoughts moving around in your mind, like the glitter is moving around in the bottle?

Now put the bottle down, so it's still. Watch what happens to the glitter. It settles to the bottom. You can do the same with your thoughts. You can just notice your thoughts and let them be. This can help your thoughts calm down, like the glitter calms down and goes to the bottom of the bottle when you let the bottle be.

 **TIP**

Practice using the glitter bottle activity to let your thoughts be. You can shake up the bottle and then watch the glitter settle. Or you can imagine what the glitter looks like when you shake up the bottle. Either way, imagine your thoughts are settling like the glitter. You could do this when it's hard to let your thoughts be; for example, when you feel worried, sad, or angry.

Texting on a Cell Phone

This activity will help you practice letting go of your thoughts and feelings. This is a quick activity you can do when your thoughts and feelings are strong. One way to let go of thoughts and feelings is to write them down.

On the next page is a picture of a cell phone. **On the screen, write some thoughts or feelings that your mind comes up with**. Try to make them look like texts. Then read the words. They can't hurt you because they're just words, made up of letters of the alphabet. Writing down your thoughts and feelings, then reminding yourself that they're just words, will help you to let go of your thoughts and feelings. Then they won't feel so strong.

How did you feel after you wrote them down? Did it feel easier to let them go?

_____

_____

_____

_____

_____

Giving Your Thoughts a Movie Title

Imagine that you made a movie about your life. This movie would include your thoughts and feelings. What title or name would you give the movie? For example: Maria called her movie "The Girl Who Worried." **Write your title on the movie screen**.

After you write down the movie title, try saying the name of the movie like you're recording a movie preview. **What else would you say about the movie?** You can even draw a picture from the movie on the screen if that helps you imagine more clearly.

_____

_____

_____

_____

_____

When it's hard to deal with your thoughts and feelings, or when they feel strong, think of what title or name you would give a movie that includes those thoughts and feelings. Then say, "Here's the movie of…," followed by the title or name. For example: "Here's the movie of 'The Girl Who Worried.'" This can help you feel less overwhelmed by your thoughts and feelings.

Imagining Cars on a Ferris Wheel

Noticing your thoughts and feelings like they are cars on a Ferris wheel can help you deal with them. You don't have to do anything to try to get rid of them. Just let them be.

Pretend that you are watching a Ferris wheel with different color cars. For example: You might notice a red car, then a blue car, then a silver car. Try to notice each car. If you start to think about other things, try to bring your mind back to watching the Ferris wheel and noticing the cars. You might like to close your eyes for this activity.

How did this activity go for you? If your mind thought about other things, were you able to bring your mind back to watching the Ferris wheel and noticing the cars?

In the picture of the Ferris wheel, write a different thought on each car. Then color or decorate each car in a way that reminds you of its thought.

Now look at your drawing and the thoughts you wrote on the cars. While you look, don't try to get rid of these thoughts. Just notice them.

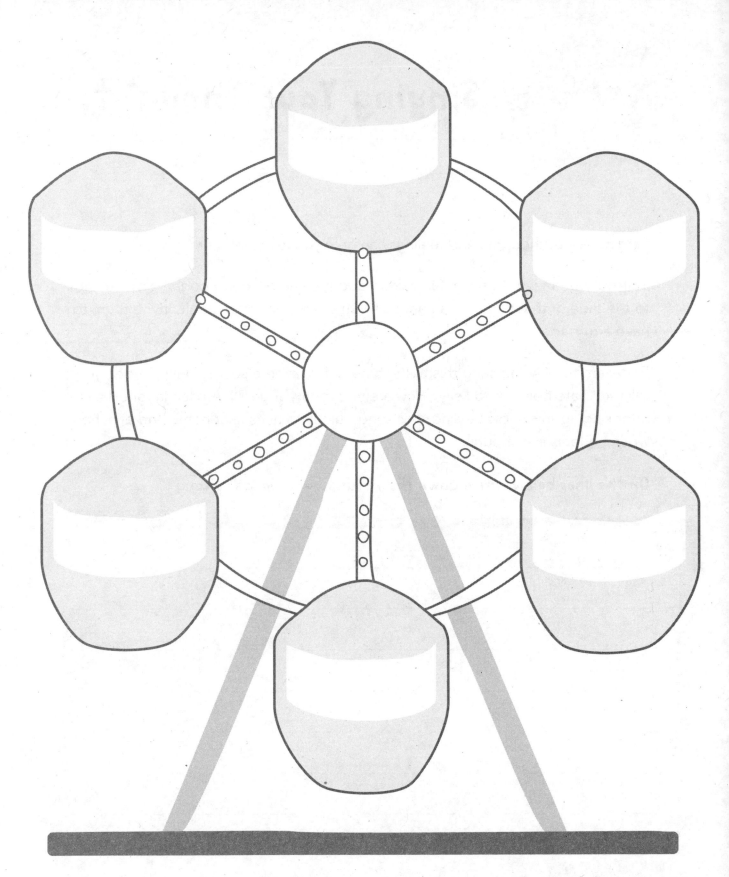

Singing Your Thoughts

Singing about thoughts and feelings can help you let go of them.

Think about a favorite song. Sing aloud about some of your thoughts and feelings to the tune of that song. If you are doing this activity with an adult, invite them to have a turn too.

For example: Aiyden sang this to the tune of his favorite song: "Hello, anger, you tell me I hate noise. And I say, 'How are you today, anger?'" Aiyden laughed a lot after singing this. Now he sings this song quietly to himself at home and at school when he feels like shouting.

On the lines below, write down the words to your made up song.

Blowing Bubbles

Now let's look at how blowing bubbles can help you to both let it be and let it go at the same time.

BLOWING BUBBLES FUN

Blowing bubbles is one of my favorite activities. You can do this with a parent, with someone else in your family, or on your own. If you blow bubbles outside, you can watch them blow away if it's windy. You can also do this activity inside.

MATERIALS

- Small bottle of bubble liquid

INSTRUCTIONS

- Try to notice what your mind is telling you. Say one thought aloud and then blow the bubbles once. Don't try to pop the bubbles. Just watch them float away.

- If you are doing this activity with someone else, take turns saying a thought aloud and then blowing the bubbles once. When you're done, think about how noticing your thoughts and letting them be might help you in the future. Is there anything that might make it hard to notice your thoughts and not do anything with them?

- If you don't have bubbles, write down your thoughts in the bubbles below. Then close your eyes and imagine those thoughts floating away.

REMINDERS:

Let It Be and Let It Go

- Notice thoughts without doing anything with them.

- Sing about thoughts and feelings to the tune of a favorite song.

- Talk to your thoughts and feelings. You can say:

  "Thanks, mind!"

  "Hello, worries!"

  "Hello, thoughts, you can come with me."

  "Hello, sadness, it's so great to see you!"

  "Hello, anger, you're looking fabulous today!"

  "Thanks, mind, for that interesting thought!"

> Hello, thoughts!

For a copy of this page to print out, visit http://www.newharbinger.com/51819

Choose What Matters and Do What Matters

We looked at using *let it be* and *let it go* in Section 2. In this section, you'll learn about *choose what matters* and *do what matters*. You'll see examples of how Maria, Aiyden, and Jia used these actions to help deal with their thoughts and feelings.

- *Choose what matters* means pick what you really care about.

- *Do what matters* means do things that you really care about. I care a lot about helping kids, so I work at a clinic and help kids deal with their thoughts and feelings.

Do any of your thoughts and feelings stop you from doing something you care about? For example: When you feel sad, you might not play with your dog, not practice playing a musical instrument, or ask your parent to cancel a playdate.

You can choose what you care about most. You can do things you care about. You can do things that you know are safe, even if your mind tells you that you feel worried, sad, or angry.

Write down some things that you care about that your thoughts and feelings have stopped you from doing:

Maria's mind worried a lot. When it worried, she stayed home. Maria missed a lot of school. Maria's parent asked her if there was anything about school she cared about. Maria said she cared a lot about playing with friends and going to math class. Thinking about these things helped Maria to go to school, even when her mind worried.

Maria's Story

I loved playing piano. But I was *really* worried about the recital. Every time I thought about it, my mind said I wouldn't do a good job. My mind said that everyone would notice and laugh when I made mistakes. My mind was saying mean things like, "You're no good at piano and shouldn't play." This made me scared. I told my parents that I wasn't going to play at the recital. Then I asked myself if there was something about playing at the recital that I cared about. My parents and friend were coming to watch me play at the recital. I didn't want to disappoint them by not playing. I also wanted to play because I had been practicing for a long time. But I thought I couldn't because I was scared. It turned out I didn't have to listen to my mind! I played in the recital and had fun. I didn't notice if I made mistakes. I felt so proud that I tried and didn't let my mind win.

Things You Care About

When your thoughts and feelings are strong, your mind might tell you that you can't do something, like go to soccer practice. Thinking about why you care about soccer practice will help you go to soccer practice.

In the hearts below, write down some things you care about. Choose smaller hearts for smaller things you care about, like eating your favorite food. Choose larger hearts for things you care about a lot, like your team winning a game.

Sometimes your thoughts and feelings are very strong and have lots of power over you. You might not feel like doing things you care about. Or you might not do them often. You can become more powerful when you do things you care about, even when your thoughts and feelings are very strong.

Jia's Visit to Her Grandparents

Jia and her family were going to her grandparents' house for her grandmother's birthday. She had made her grandmother a card and really wanted to give it to her. Jia's dog, Scout, had died, and she missed him a lot. Her mind told her she was too sad to go. She cared a lot about seeing her grandmother on her birthday. So even though her mind told her she was too sad and wouldn't have a good time, Jia went anyway. Her grandmother was very happy when Jia gave her the card she made. Jia was happy she had visited her grandparents.

Magic Wand

Your thoughts and feelings don't have to stop you from doing things you care about. When you feel sad, worried, or angry, try pretending that you have a magic wand that can help you do things you care about or do them more often.

Write down some thoughts and feelings that have been stopping you from doing things you care about.

_____

_____

_____

_____

_____

Write down some things you have stopped doing because of your thoughts and feelings.

_____

_____

_____

_____

_____

Color in this picture of a magic wand and decorate it anyway you'd like.

ACTIVITY
19

Schedule for Doing Things You Care About

It can be hard to do things you care about when feelings like worry, sadness, or anger get in the way. Making a schedule for doing some things that you care about can help. For example, you might want to walk your dog, play a musical instrument, celebrate family birthdays, or spend time outside. Writing down things you want to do on a schedule makes it more likely that you'll do them. This helps you plan ahead. Then you will feel less stressed and overwhelmed.

You can also schedule new things you'd like to try or things you have stopped doing because of your feelings and would like to do again. For example, you might want to do a new activity or return to one you stopped doing.

SUNDAY	MONDAY	TUESDAY	WEDNESDAY	THURSDAY	FRIDAY	SATURDAY
	SCIENCE EXHIBIT	⭐ Walk Buster				⭐ HIKE WITH DAD
Lucy's Birthday Party						VISIT GRANDMA
⭐ MOVIE NIGHT!		DANCE TRYOUTS	⭐ Walk Buster	PRACTICE VIOLIN		

FILL OUT A WEEK'S SCHEDULE

On the next page is a week's schedule for you to fill out. You might want to ask your parent to help you schedule things around other activities that you have. If you want, you can also ask your parent to help you (or remind you to) stick to your schedule even when it's hard.

- Write some things on the schedule that you do that you care about and want to do no matter how you feel.

- Next, think about some new things you'd like to try or some things you have stopped doing because of your feelings and would like to do again. Write some of these things in the schedule.

- As you fill out the schedule, think about what feelings get in the way of each thing you want to do. What can you do to deal with those feelings? If you'd like, add some notes to the schedule to remind you about ways to deal with those feelings. Add a note to follow the schedule, even when your feelings are very strong.

Be kind to yourself and try to do something you care about every few days. Remind yourself what it is you love or enjoy about doing those things.

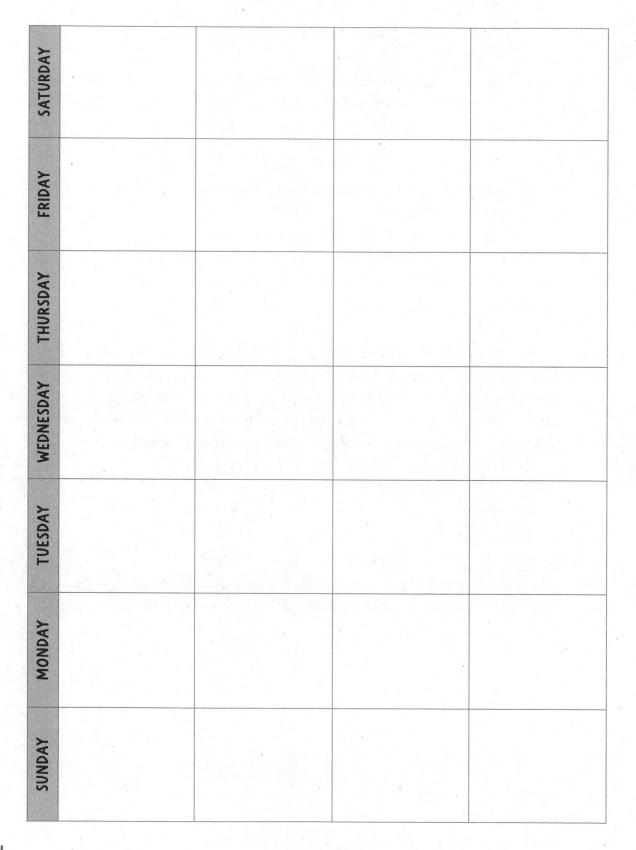

Aiyden's Choices

Aiyden's thoughts and feelings were so strong that he believed everything his mind told him. Sometimes he made choices that didn't help him. Then he felt even worse. Let's look at a quiz about the things Aiyden could do to help himself.

Circle the answers to the two questions below that you think would help Aiyden the most. When you finish, you can look at the answers on the next page. But don't look at them until after you have finished doing this quiz.

1. A child in Aiyden's class invites Aiyden to his party at an indoor rock-climbing center. Aiyden wants to go to the party because he wants to have fun with other kids. But he is worried it might be noisy. Aiyden could:

   a. Stay home because the party might be noisy.

   b. Go to the party and try rock climbing. If he starts feeling annoyed that it's noisy, he can say to himself, "Hi, annoyed, it's great to see you!" Then he can keep going with rock climbing, because he cares about having fun with other kids.

   c. Ask the kid who is having the party if he can make sure there's no noise at the party.

   d. Go to the party. But if it's noisy, refuse to rock climb and sit in the corner being very angry.

2. At recess at school, Aiyden wants to play a game with other kids. He could:

a. Tell some kids what game he wants to play.

b. Go up to a group of kids who are already playing a game and try to change the game to what he wants to play.

c. Ask some kids if they would like to play a game and let them choose. If they choose a game he doesn't like, he can remind himself that he cares about playing with other kids, and let his feelings be of not liking the game. Then he can play the game they chose.

d. Wait for kids to invite him to play with them.

Here are the answers that would best help Aiyden.

1. The best answer is (b): Go to the party and try rock climbing. If he starts feeling annoyed that it's noisy, he can say to himself, "Hi, annoyed, it's great to see you!" Then he can keep going with rock climbing, because he cares about having fun with other kids.

2. The best answer is (c): Ask some kids if they would like to play a game and let them choose. If they choose a game he doesn't like, he can remind himself that he cares about playing with other kids, and let his feelings be of not liking the game. Then he can play the game they chose.

Making a Treasure Box

Imagine that you are going to spend a week on a beautiful island and are taking some things you care about in a special treasure box. In this activity, you'll make a treasure box that holds special items or photos of special items.

Think about what's in your treasure box when you are having difficulty dealing with your thoughts and feelings. It can help to open your treasure box and remind yourself of what you care about. This can help you do things even when your mind tells you that you feel worried, sad, or angry. For example, a new friend invites you to their house. You feel worried because you haven't been to their house before and don't know what to expect. You look in your treasure box and remember that you care about spending time with friends and having fun with them. You go to your new friend's house and enjoy yourself.

Fill with special things you care about.

TREASURE BOX

HOW TO MAKE A TREASURE BOX

Start by thinking about some things that are special to you (for example, a photo of your pet, or your favorite book or toy).

MATERIALS

- A cardboard box, such as an empty shoebox

- Plain paper to cover the box if it has writing or pictures on it

- Tape to stick the paper to the box, if needed

- Colored markers

- Things to decorate the box, such as stickers

INSTRUCTIONS

- If the box has writing or pictures on it, tape paper on it to cover the outside. If you'd like, you can paint the paper and once it's dry, cover the box with it.

- Put some things that you care about inside the box. Or take photos of things you care about. Print the photos and put them inside the box. (You may need help from a parent if you're using photos.)

- Draw on the outside of your treasure box with the markers and add decorations, such as stickers, if you'd like.

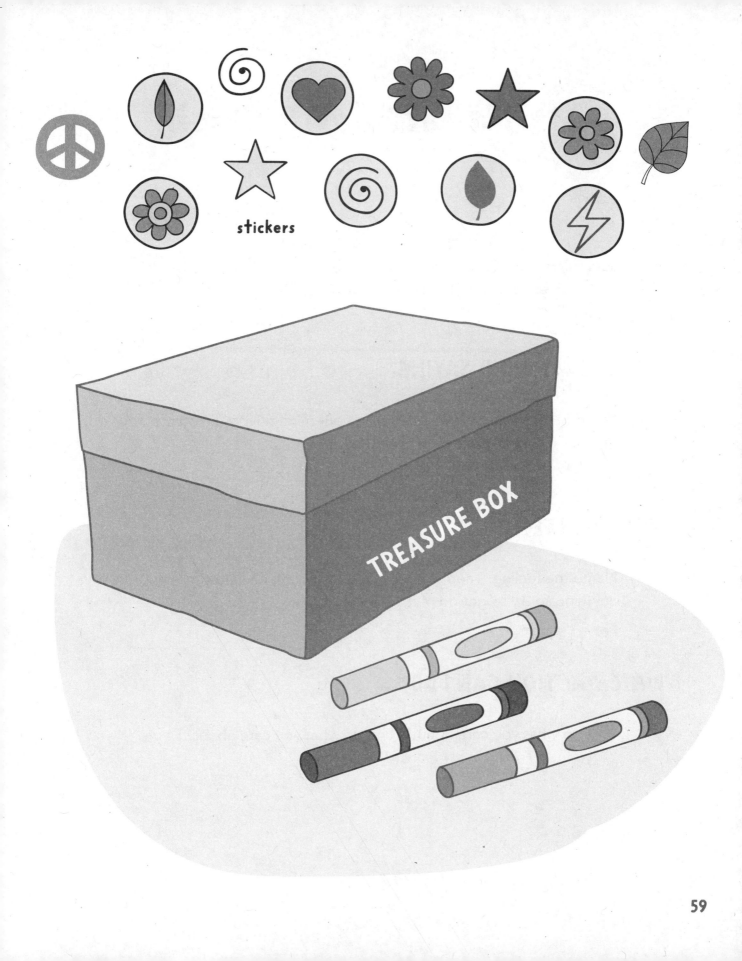

stickers

TREASURE BOX

What? How? Which?

When your mind says that you are worried, sad, angry, or have another strong feeling, you can ask yourself these three questions:

WHAT IS MY MIND SAYING?

- You don't have to believe everything your mind tells you! You can let your thoughts be and let them go.

HOW AM I FEELING?

- Name the feeling. Then say hello to it. You don't have to do anything to try to get rid of it.

WHICH ACTION CAN I DO?

- Choose what you care about. Then do what you care about.

Read the statements in the following tables and fill in the blank spaces.
You can use what you've already learned in this book to help you decide which actions you can take. Doing this activity will help you identify your thoughts and feelings and what causes them. It will also help you develop an action plan.

WHAT IS MY MIND SAYING?	HOW AM I FEELING?	WHICH ACTION CAN I DO?
Everyone will laugh if I ask a question in class.	Worried	I can say to myself, "Hello, worried, how are you today?" I can put my hand up and ask a question, even if my mind says everyone will laugh.
I have no one to play with at recess at school.	Lonely	
	Angry	
I can't do my homework. It's too hard!		
	Disappointed	

WHAT IS MY MIND SAYING?	HOW AM I FEELING?	WHICH ACTION CAN I DO?
I always mess things up.		
It's too scary to go on a field trip somewhere new.		
	Sad	
	Embarrassed	

62

WHAT IS MY MIND SAYING?	HOW AM I FEELING?	WHICH ACTION CAN I DO?

Word Search

This word search contains some words that you've seen in this section on choose what matters and do what matters. Try finding the words listed below to help you remember what you learned in this section.

AIYDEN	HEART	MATTERS
BOX	HOW	START
DOING	JIA	THOUGHTS
DRAW	MAGIC WAND	TRYING
FEELINGS	MARIA	WHAT
		WHICH

Circle the words listed below or color them with a light marker. Hint: Words are shown horizontally (across), vertically (downward), and diagonally (on an angle).

```
            C P H K                    M G D Y
          T W M S A M                D U C M R I
        S H H M M K E N            Y N B A A M A S
    S G O I K S F I J Q      D W N P I R U U W X
    N U U C C Y T Y E W Y H V O X Y I S R W Z
    E V G H S C R N Y F M D C H D D A T B H G
    F X H J D M D O I N G N U M S E R A P A J
    L Q T Q K X T F F E M W F A E N U R R T P
    P O S J Q B R I E T Q R D T W U G T T A I
      F K P G Z Y A P E J V B T P G X M D R
      B M R L C I Y C B L I D E N B Q O K K
        C A O Z N I X H I I A R I E O R U
        C H G M G E B O U W N S B S Q X O
          T E I N E F W Y N U G L H Q Q
          L A C M S V B O X A S J Y
            D R W M H R O J I A K
            D T A N O C I S R
            K L N Y Q O U
              T A D D P
              U L Y
              S
```

Choose What Matters and Do What Matters

- What do you care about most?

- What do you do that you really care about?

- What are some new things you could do that you care about? What are things you have stopped doing that you could start doing again?

- When could you try doing things you care about?

- Ask yourself: What is my mind saying? How am I feeling? Which action can I do?

- Try to do something you care about every few days.

Stay Here and Notice Yourself

In this section, you're going to learn about *stay here* and *notice yourself*. You'll learn how Maria, Aiyden, and Jia used these actions to help themselves deal with their thoughts and feelings.

When your mind is busy thinking or your feelings are very strong, it's hard to focus on what's happening around you. You may not notice someone calling your name or talking to you. You might ride in a car or bus and not notice where you are. You might eat but not notice how foods taste. Do any of these things ever happen to you? Also, when you feel worried, sad, angry, or another strong feeling, you might do things that make you feel even worse.

When you pay attention to what's happening around you and notice what you're doing, your thoughts and feelings are less powerful.

STAY HERE

Stay here means paying attention to where you are right now and what's happening. It can be a very good way to deal with your thoughts and feelings. It will also help you concentrate better and calm your mind and your body.

Remember in Section 2 when you made the glitter bottle? You noticed the water becoming calm and the glitter settling. Using stay here can help your thoughts and feelings settle. Then they don't feel as big and strong, and your mind doesn't feel as powerful.

Aiyden's Story

I practice staying here each morning when I brush my teeth. I focus on how the brush handle feels in my hand. I smell the toothpaste. I feel the brush and toothpaste in my mouth. Sometimes I think about what I'm going to do that day, like going to school and playing sports. But then I come back to focusing on brushing my teeth. Practicing staying here has helped me concentrate better. Now I am aware when I start feeling angry. Then I practice staying here. This helps me calm down.

NOTICE YOURSELF

Notice yourself means watching yourself doing things. It's like looking in a mirror, but you don't need an actual mirror to notice yourself. You can notice yourself reading, sitting in class, eating, bathing, doing homework, playing, watching TV, lying in bed, and doing lots of other things.

Stay here and notice what you're doing right now. The more you stay here, the easier it is to notice yourself. The more you notice yourself, the easier it is to stay here. Let's try some activities first to practice staying here and then do the same for noticing yourself.

Jia's Story

When Jia was sad at home, she went to her bedroom. She laid on her bed until she felt better. She thought that no one understood how she felt. Jia felt lonely and alone. Sometimes Jia was in her bedroom for a long time.

Then Jia practiced noticing herself. She noticed when she was sad, and what she was doing. She noticed that being by herself when she was sad didn't make her feel less sad.

At home, instead of staying in her bedroom until she felt better, Jia started telling her parents or her sister how she felt, and she spent time with them. At school, Jia noticed that she didn't speak to other people when she was sad, and this made her feel worse. Then, she spoke to other kids and teachers, and she noticed herself doing this. When Jia practiced noticing herself, she was able to chose actions that helped her feel better.

Floppy Octopus

This activity will help you pay attention to moving and how you feel in your body. It will also help you notice your thoughts and feelings.

Start by sitting in a chair or lying on the floor or carpet. You may want to close your eyes. Ask your parent to read these words aloud to you:

Imagine that you are a floppy octopus swimming under the sea. The waves are big, and you move with them. Imagine you are flopping around in the water. Maybe your legs are moving from side to side, and your arms are moving up and down. Then the waves slow down. The sea becomes very calm. The water hardly moves at all. See if you can now be very still, like an octopus resting on the sand on the bottom of the sea. Now notice yourself being very still and calm. Notice how that feels in your body. Notice what you are thinking and feeling.

The floppy octopus activity might help you deal with your thoughts and feelings when you feel worried, sad, angry, or some other strong feeling. No matter what you are feeling, that feeling will eventually go away, like a wave that calms down in the sea.

Write down what you noticed when you tried this activity.

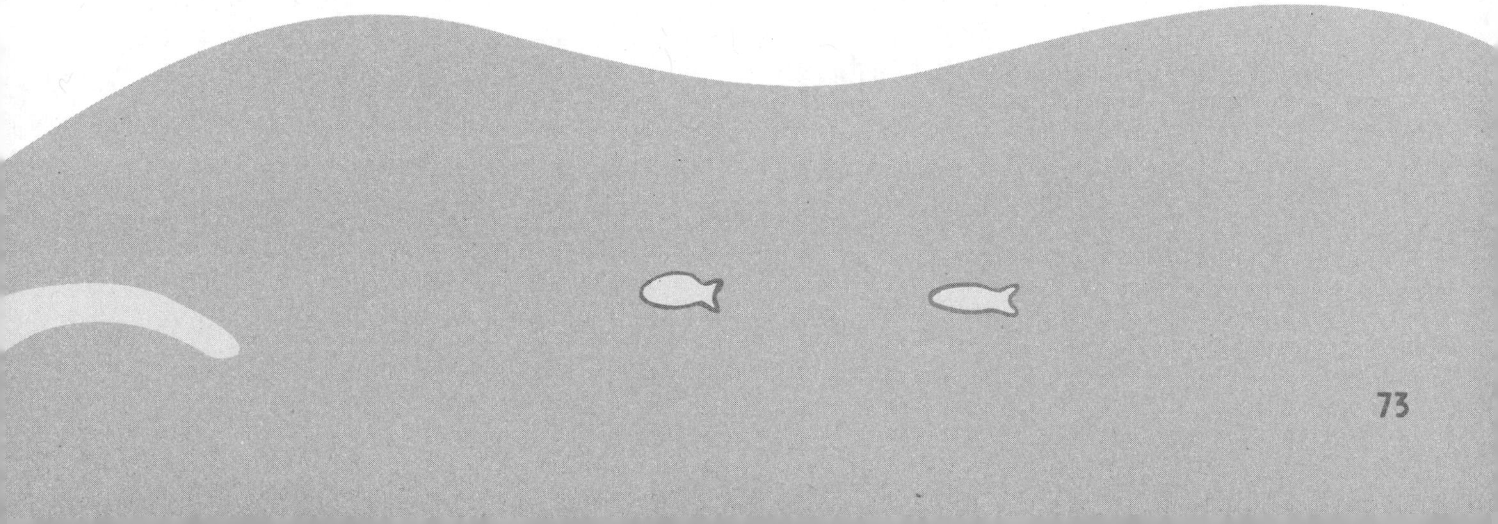

_____

_____

_____

_____

_____

_____

_____

_____

Staying Here While Eating

Try staying here while eating. You might like to practice with a piece of fruit, raisins, or something else.

First read the following instructions, which will help you practice staying here while eating. Do your best to remember them as you practice on your own. If you'd like help, you can ask your parent to read them aloud to you as you practice.

Take one bite. Pay attention to what is happening in your mouth. Notice the taste of the food. Don't rush. Take one bite at a time. Note how the taste changes. Note how your teeth and tongue work. See if you can notice when you feel like you need to swallow. Then feel how the food moves down your throat as you swallow. After you have swallowed, when you are ready, take another bite. Take your time. Notice how your body, mind, and heart feel at this moment.

Now try answering these questions about the food you chose:

What colors can you see in the food? _____

Does the food have a smell? _____

What does the food taste like? _____

Is it crunchy or chewy? _____

Does it taste sweet or sour? _____

Is the food hot or cold? _____

Maria's Story

I had a lot of fun learning how to stay here while eating. My parent and I practiced with dried fruits. It was like tasting these fruits for the very first time! This activity taught me to slow down and notice the smell and color of the fruits. I also noticed the way the fruits felt on my tongue. Then I practiced it at school during lunch. Now I try to practice every day. I also remind my family to practice when we're eating dinner. It's helped me focus on what's going on around me. I can concentrate better now. When I get worried, I practice staying here. Then my worries don't seem so big. Sometimes, I don't even notice when my mind worries!

ACTIVITY 26

Staying Here While Breathing

This breathing activity will help you to stay here and feel calmer. It will also help your feelings settle. You can do it whenever you feel worried, sad, angry, or another strong feeling. You can do it at home, at school, or anywhere else.

- Sit, stand, or lie down, depending on where you are.

- Close your eyes, if you'd like. If you want to leave your eyes open, choose a spot on the floor or the ceiling to look at. Try to look at the same spot for the whole activity, instead of looking around.

- Put your hands flat on the sides of your belly.

- Take a couple of slow breaths. Breathe in through your nose. Slowly breathe out through your mouth.

- Continue to breathe slowly in through your nose and out through your mouth. Feel your belly gently going in and then going out. It's like a balloon being blown up and then having its air let out.

- Continue as long as you'd like.

Staying Here While Falling Asleep

You can practice this activity when you get into bed at night to help you fall asleep.

Once you've settled in bed, practice staying here by focusing on what you hear.

- Close your eyes.

- Listen to the sounds inside your room.

- Then listen to the sounds outside your room.

- Finally, listen to the sound of your breathing.

If it's hard to remember to practice this in bed at night, you can make a sign to remind you. You might like to decorate the sign, then put it near your bed.

Jia's Story

I used to have a dog named Scout, but he died. I missed Scout a lot when I went to bed at night. I thought about how he always ran into my bedroom in the morning, wagging his tail. He used to jump up on my bed. Then I cuddled him. It was hard to fall asleep because I felt sad. Practicing staying here when I went to bed helped me fall asleep more quickly.

Imagining a Stop Sign

When your thoughts and feelings feel very strong, imagine a big sign that says **STOP**. Just like people stop driving to look both ways when they see a stop sign, you can stop to notice your emotions.

For example: When you feel angry at someone or about something, you might do things that aren't helpful and make things worse. Instead, imagine a stop sign and ask yourself:

- Am I making things better or worse?

- What can I do instead?

Write down an example of when noticing yourself might help you deal with your thoughts and feelings.

_____

_____

_____

_____

_____

_____

_____

_____

How Aiyden Used Stay Here and Notice Yourself

Remember how Aiyden was often angry? He shouted at home and at school. People were scared of him. Aiyden learned to stop before he got too angry and thought about what he wanted to do instead.

   At first, Aiyden noticed himself wanting to call out in class. Then he put up his hand instead. His teacher told him he was doing a great job. The other students began inviting Aiyden to play at lunch. He noticed himself feeling upset when he didn't get to choose the game. He decided to notice the playground, the trees, and the other students instead. This helped Aiyden. He did not shout, and Aiyden and the other students had fun playing together.

ACTIVITY 29

Feelings Mountain

This activity can help you notice when your feelings become stronger and settle them down.

Sometimes your feelings aren't very strong when they begin. But they can become stronger and stronger. Things might happen that worry you, make you sad, or make you angry. These feelings can often become even stronger.

Imagine a "feelings" mountain that has levels numbered 0 to 10. At the bottom of the mountain is 0, which means that the feeling is settled. The higher you climb, the stronger your feelings become and the higher the number gets. When you reach the top, your feelings are strongest, which you would rate a 10.

Think about a recent time when you felt a 10. Using the mountain figure on the next page, describe the emotions you felt at each stage. **Next to 10, describe your strongest feelings. Next to 9, describe your feelings a little less strong than 10. Do this for each number on the mountain.**

When you first notice yourself becoming sad, worried, angry, or another strong feeling, try to imagine where you are on your feelings mountain. Give it a number on a scale of 0 to 10. Wherever you are, imagine that you've stopped climbing so your feelings don't become stronger. Then let your feelings be. Next imagine yourself climbing down the mountain, letting go of your feelings and picturing them becoming less strong as you go down.

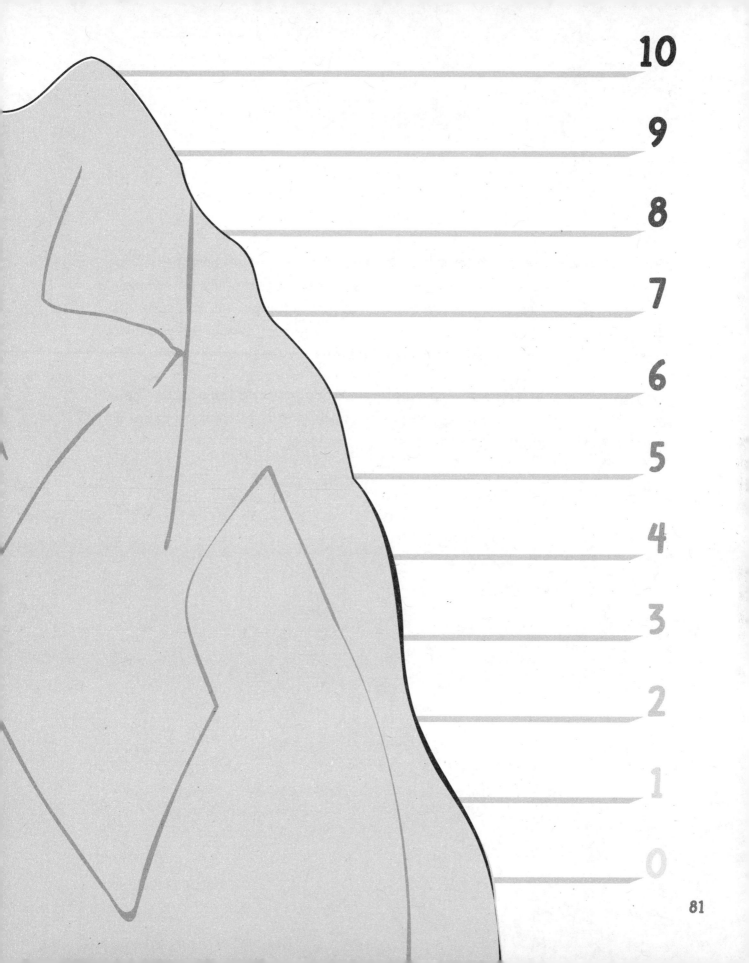

10

9

8

7

6

5

4

3

2

1

0

81

Under the Sea

The sea has waves of different sizes. It also has sand, seaweed, and shells. The sea is home to lots of living creatures, like fish, seaweed, dolphins, and whales. These are part of the sea. Just like the sea has lots of things in it, you have lots of different thoughts and feelings inside you. These are part of you. But you don't have the same thoughts and feelings all the time.

On this drawing of the sea, write different thoughts and feelings on the waves. You might like to draw a treasure box under the sea that holds things you care about, or anything else that you'd like to include.

ACTIVITY 31

Riding in a Hot Air Balloon

This activity will help you practice noticing yourself. Sit down and ask your parent to read the following aloud to you. You can close your eyes or choose a spot on the floor to look at while you listen.

Imagine you are riding in a hot air balloon, high up in the sky. You look down and see yourself feeling worried, sad, angry, or another strong feeling. You might be at home, at school, or somewhere else. Notice what you are doing to try to deal with your thoughts and feelings. Notice any thoughts and feelings that your mind comes up with while you watch yourself from the hot air balloon.

Did you see yourself doing anything that surprised you? Do you think what you do to try to deal with your thoughts and feelings helps you?

_____

_____

_____

_____

Next to the picture of the hot air balloon, write some thoughts and other feelings you have when you feel worried, sad, or angry.

Think about what you've read in this book that you could use when you feel worried, sad, or angry. **Write some things you could do that might help you.**

_____

_____

_____

_____

_____

ACTIVITY 32

Leaves on a Tree

Trees have a trunk and branches. Sometimes the branches are full of leaves. Leaves are part of the tree, but they are not the whole tree. Sometimes you have lots of thoughts and feelings. Other times you have fewer. Your thoughts and feelings are like leaves on a tree. They are part of you, but they are not all of you. There are lots more things about you!

When you feel worried, sad, angry, or another strong feeling, try noticing your thoughts and feelings. Remind yourself that they are a part of you, but they are not all of you.

On the tree, draw leaves on the branches. Make the leaves large enough to write inside them. Then write some of your thoughts and feelings inside the leaves.

Still, Quiet Ship

This activity uses imagining and will help you stop, let go of your thoughts, and notice what you are doing. When you feel worried, sad, or angry, noticing yourself can help you to stop and see what actions you are doing. You can ask yourself if your actions are helping you. Then you can change your actions if they aren't helping you. You can do actions that are more helpful.

You can practice this activity any time your thoughts and feelings are strong—at home, school, or somewhere else. You could ask your parent to read the instructions to you and close your eyes while you are listening. Or you could read the instructions yourself, then close your eyes.

Pretend that you are in a very big ship that is heavy and safe in the water. Even though there are waves, the ship is still and quiet. It's stormy outside. There are lots of dark clouds in the sky. Imagine that your thoughts are the storm clouds. You can watch them safely from inside the ship. Each time your mind comes up with a thought, place it on a storm cloud. Watch the storm clouds and notice what they look like. Notice yourself, inside a ship, watching the storm clouds. **Then write some of your thoughts on the storm clouds on the next page.**

Stay Here and Notice Yourself

- Your thoughts and feelings are a part of you, but they are not all of you.

- Put your hands on the sides of your belly. Breathe in slowly through your nose and out through your mouth. Feel your belly gently going in and out.

- Practice staying here for things you do every day, like brushing your teeth and eating.

- Your thoughts and feelings change. They don't stay the same all the time.

- Notice what you are thinking and feeling. Then practice not doing everything your mind tells you to do, like not yelling when your mind tells you to.

- When your thoughts and feelings feel very strong, imagine seeing a big sign that says *STOP!* Then ask yourself if you are making things better or worse.

- Imagine you are in a ship and your thoughts are storm clouds you watch from inside the ship. Place each thought on a storm cloud. Watch the clouds and notice yourself watching.

For a copy of this page to print out, visit http://www.newharbinger.com/51819

Be Kind and Caring to Yourself

In this section, you'll look at *being kind and caring to yourself*. You'll learn how Maria, Aiyden, and Jia used these actions to help them deal with their thoughts and feelings.

When you speak to yourself, it can sometimes be hard to be kind and caring. Your mind may be mean to you or tell you off. Your mind may say that you aren't doing things well enough or that you aren't trying hard enough. When you feel worried, sad, angry, or another strong feeling, speaking to yourself in a mean or unkind way often makes you feel even worse.

When you speak to people you care a lot about, such as family and friends, you likely speak to them in a kind and caring way. When you speak to yourself in a kind and caring way, your thoughts and feelings become less powerful. Then you can often deal with them better.

BE KIND AND CARING TO YOURSELF

Be kind and caring to yourself means using nice words when you speak to yourself. It also means taking good care of yourself and reminding yourself that you are trying your best. You can also say something to yourself like "good try" or "good job" when you try and do things that you find difficult. This will help you to keep trying and become calmer.

Activities in this section will help you practice being kind and caring to yourself.

Maria's Story

I was very worried about playing the piano in my recital. I was scared of making mistakes. My mind was mean to me. My mind said that I wasn't good at playing piano and that I hadn't practiced enough. When this happened, I told myself that piano is difficult for me, and I was trying my best. I also had practiced hard to play in the recital. During the recital, when I felt nervous, I told myself I was doing really well. This helped me calm down. After the recital, I told myself that I had done a great job, and I felt proud.

ACTIVITY 34

Kind and Caring Statements Jar

Have you ever had a coach who spoke to you or your team in a very kind and caring way? Perhaps the coach noticed that you or the team tried really hard and were doing a great job. Think about what a kind and caring coach might say to you. This activity will help you remember these statements.

HOW TO MAKE A KIND AND CARING STATEMENTS JAR

For this activity, you're going to write kind and caring statements and fill a jar with them.

MATERIALS

- Plastic or glass jar

- Pieces of paper in different colors

- Colored markers

- Plain sticker label, glue, or tape

KINDNESS JAR

INSTRUCTIONS

- Cut up strips of paper, using a few different colors. Make the strips big enough to write a sentence or two on.

- On each strip of paper, write down what a kind and caring coach might say to you. Use one strip of paper per statement. Put the strips of paper in the jar.

- If you have a label, write a name for the jar on it and decorate it with the markers. Stick the label on the outside of the jar. If you don't have a label, write on and decorate a strip of paper. Use glue or tape to stick it on the jar.

When you feel worried, sad, angry, or another strong feeling, take out some of the strips and read them to yourself. Then put them back in the jar.

Aiyden's Story

Sometimes I get angry very quickly. Then my body feels hot, and my face gets red. I feel like a volcano about to explode! When this happens, I imagine that a kind and caring coach is talking to me. This helps me calm down. Then I tell myself that I am okay and that I did very well calming myself down. I feel proud when I can calm myself.

Giving a Speech About Someone You Care About

Imagine that you are going to give a speech at someone's party you care a lot about. This could be a family member, a friend, someone else, or your pet. Think about what kind and caring words you could use. Imagine how you feel saying those words. Pretend that they are very pleased with your speech. They tell you how much they care about you. Notice how it feels in your body to be told this.

Whenever you feel worried, sad, angry, or another strong feeling, you can recreate this feeling by imagining giving this speech. Then imagine the person telling you how much they care about you and notice how your body feels.

Write a kind and caring speech about someone you care about in the space below.

_____

_____

_____

_____

_____

_____

_____

Letter Reminders

Create a three-word saying that will help you practice being kind and caring to yourself. Write the first letter of each word in the squares below. For example: "You Got This" (Y-G-T) or "You're Doing Well" (Y-D-W). Pick your favorite saying and write the letters large in the squares below. You can color or decorate the squares any way you like. Then, on the line above the squares, write down when it might be helpful to use your three-word saying.

Y   G   T   You got this!

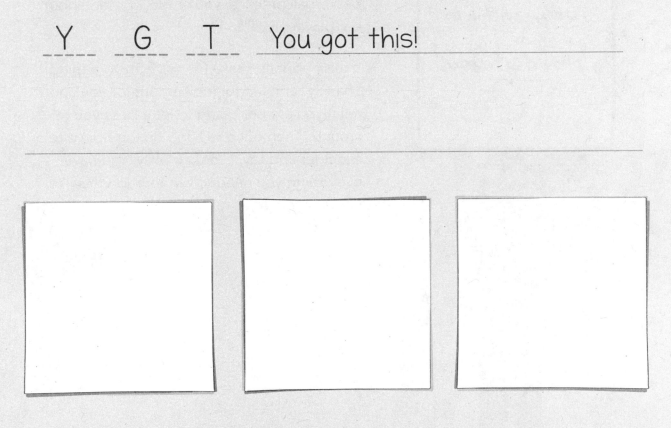

ACTIVITY
37

Making Friends with Your Mind

You are okay. I'm here for you, and I'm proud of you.

Sometimes it might feel like your mind has lots of power over you. This can happen when your feelings are very strong, and you believe everything your mind says. For example, your mind might say, "Don't go to school, your stomach hurts" or "Don't go to basketball practice, you're too worried about not playing well."

If this happens, make friends with your mind. Thank your mind for looking out for you and tell it you are not going to let it boss you around. Then put one hand on the opposite shoulder and say, "You are okay. You have everything you need to get through this. I'm here for you, and I'm proud of you."

In the space below, draw a picture of yourself making friends with your mind.

GOOD JOB!

ACTIVITY 38

Imagining a Calm and Peaceful Place

Close your eyes and imagine a place where you feel calm and peaceful. This might be your bedroom, your yard, the beach, woods, a place with animals, or somewhere else. Notice how your body and mind feel imagining this place. Whenever you feel worried, sad, angry, or another strong feeling, you can imagine this place. You can imagine this place any time you want to, when you are at home, school, or elsewhere. When you do, practice talking to yourself in a kind and caring way.

Jia's Story

Sometimes I feel sad about my dog, Scout, who died. When this happens, I close my eyes and think about going to the beach. I imagine that I'm collecting shells, building sandcastles, and swimming in the ocean. This helps me feel calm. Then I tell myself it's all right to feel sad about missing Scout, and I'm going to be okay.

If you'd like, color in the image with colored markers, pencils, or crayons to make it look as peaceful as possible.

103

ACTIVITY 39

Thoughts, Feelings, and Actions

Think about something that you are worried, sad, or angry about and write it down in the "Situation" column of the table below. Next write down what you're thinking in the "Thought" column and what you're feeling in the "Feeling" column. Then answer the three questions in the table. I've provided an example.

Fill in the blank spaces for other situations you think you will have difficulty with. You might like to ask your parent to help you with this activity.

SITUATION	THOUGHT	FEELING	WHAT COULD YOU DO?	WHAT MIGHT HAPPEN?	HOW COULD I SPEAK TO MYSELF IN A KIND AND CARING WAY?
Going on a school field trip somewhere new.	I don't know what to expect.	Worried	Go on the field trip. My worries can come with me.	I will have fun with my friends and learn interesting. things. I'll be glad I went!	It's okay to feel worried. Nothing bad is going to happen to me. I have gone on field trips before. I will be okay!

In the future, you can draw your own table to help you with situations you think you will have difficulty with. Include blank spaces for you to write in. Use the same headings as this one. Filling in the table will help you develop an action plan. It will also help you talk to yourself in a kind and caring way.

SITUATION	THOUGHT	FEELING

WHAT COULD YOU DO?	WHAT MIGHT HAPPEN?	HOW COULD I SPEAK TO MYSELF IN A KIND AND CARING WAY?

Word Search

The word search below contains some words that you've seen in this section on be kind and caring to yourself. Try finding the words to help you remember what you learned in this section.

ACTIONS	GOOD JOB	POWER
CALM	IMAGINE	SPEECH
CARING	KEEP GOING	THOUGHT
COACH	KIND	WELL DONE
FEELING	MIND	YOU GOT THIS
	PEACEFUL	

Circle the words below or color them with a light marker. Hint: The words are shown horizontally (across), vertically (downward), and diagonally (on an angle).

```
            R D W Z I   F R F
          G K N S I F S R S T R H
          G O O D J O B H G J T H O F
        D S L H     B K M C     G O Q W
      Z J Z W P     Y Q O A     X O U X X
      E O F A O     S P Q R     T W E G C
    W G A U X W     B W U I     K W Q C H N
    E C I C U E     O B H N     A Y F T M T
    L A O M T R     H H E G     A W J J C K
    L Q X A A I O K S K E E P G O I N G A Z
    D U Y A C G O W Z P T F M O X Q Z A L E
    O M G A N H I N C R E F E E L I N G M Z
    N I N   J K B N S M M E P M E Z   V B J
    E N C   D K N E D A E C U I     I B Q
    D T I   K I N D T R Z H       G E K
    Z M D N                   Y N T J
      Z N P B               Z B M L
        B N P E A C E F U L W N L T
        F H Y O U G O T T H I S
        R T F E P Q K Q
```

Be Kind and Caring to Yourself

- When you try to do things that you find difficult, tell yourself *well done, good try,* or *good job* afterward.

- Imagine a kind and caring coach. What would they say when you or the team are trying really hard?

- What would someone who cares about you say in a speech about you?

YOU GOT THIS!

- Think of a saying that will help you practice being kind and caring to yourself, like "You got this."

- Make friends with your mind. Put one hand on the opposite shoulder and say, "You are okay, you will get through this, and I'm proud of you!"

- Imagine a calm and quiet place where you feel peaceful. Then talk to yourself in a kind and caring way.

- When you feel sad, worried, or angry, ask yourself what you could do, what might happen, and how you could speak to yourself in a kind and caring way.

For a copy of this page to print out, visit http://www.newharbinger.com/51819

Putting It All Together

In this book, you've learned new ways to deal with your thoughts and feelings. These actions include learning how to:

- Let it be and let it go (Section 2)

- Choose what matters and do what matters (Section 3)

- Stay here and notice yourself (Section 4)

- Be kind and caring to yourself (Section 5)

This section helps you put all that learning together. Here are two more activities that you can do to help you deal with your thoughts and feelings.

Building Your Team

Think about who you can ask for support when you are having difficulty dealing with your thoughts and feelings. This might be a parent or someone else in your family, a friend, a teacher, or another person. It's good to have a few people you can ask for help in case someone isn't available. You don't have to deal with your thoughts and feelings by yourself. Especially when your thoughts and feelings are very strong. It's okay to ask for help!

Think of five people you could ask to help you when you are feeling worried, sad, angry, or another strong feeling, and write their names in the space provided. Doing this activity will help you develop a support team. When you want support for dealing with your thoughts and feelings, you'll know who you want to ask.

YOUR TEAM

_____

_____

_____

_____

_____

Your Coping Toolkit

Look through this book and choose some actions that you think will help you deal with your thoughts and feelings the most.

Put a check next to the tools that were the most helpful so you can use this page to remind you in the future.

○ "How Much You Care" Ruler
○ When Do Your Thoughts and Feelings Show Up?
○ Your Body Map
○ What Do Your Feelings Look Like?
○ Don't Think About "Ice Cream"
○ Leaving Your Thoughts Alone
○ Inviting Your Thoughts and Feelings
○ Saying Hello to Your Thoughts and Feelings
○ Making a Glitter Bottle
○ Texting on a Cell Phone
○ Giving Your Thoughts a Movie Title
○ Imagining Cars on a Ferris Wheel
○ Singing Your Thoughts
○ Blowing Bubbles
○ Things You Care About
○ Magic Wand
○ Schedule for Doing Things You Care About
○ Making a Treasure Box
○ What? How? Which?
○ Floppy Octopus
○ Staying Here While Eating
○ Staying Here While Breathing
○ Staying Here While Falling Asleep
○ Imagining a Stop Sign
○ Feelings Mountain
○ Under the Sea
○ Riding in a Hot Air Balloon
○ Leaves on a Tree
○ Still, Quiet Ship
○ Kind and Caring Statements Jar
○ Giving a Speech about Someone You Care About
○ Letter Reminders
○ Making Friends with Your Mind
○ Imagining a Calm and Peaceful Place
○ Thoughts, Feelings, and Actions
○ Building Your Team

Goodbye and Good Luck!

Now that you've finished reading this book and doing the activities, you have lots of new skills to help you deal with your thoughts and feelings. You can come back and read this book again whenever you want to. Or you can think about the activities and choose one or two at a time to practice.

You might like to print the Reminder pages and put them up in your room. (Copies to print are available at http://www.newharbinger.com/51819.) Reading them will remind you of what you've learned. You can use these actions when you feel sad, worried, angry, or some other strong feeling.

I recommend that you try to practice these new skills two or three times every week. This will help you get better at using them and also remembering to use them.

Good luck!

References

Black, T. D. 2022. *ACT for Treating Children: The Essential Guide to Acceptance and Commitment Therapy for Kids*. Oakland, CA: New Harbinger Publications.

Gilbert, P. 2009. *The Compassionate Mind: A New Approach to Life Challenges*. London: Constable.

Harris, R. 2009. *ACT Made Simple: An Easy-to-Read Primer on Acceptance and Commitment Therapy*. Oakland, CA: New Harbinger Publications.

Harris, R. 2007. *The Happiness Trap: Stop Struggling, Start Living*. Wollombi, NSW, Australia: Exisle Publishing.

Hayes, S. C., and S. Smith. 2005. *Get Out of Your Mind and Into Your Life: The New Acceptance and Commitment Therapy*. Oakland, CA: New Harbinger Publications.

Hayes, S. C., K. D. Strosahl, and K. G. Wilson. 1999. *Acceptance and Commitment Therapy: An Experiential Approach to Behavior Change*. New York: Guilford Press.

Twohig, M. P. "ACT for Anxiety Disorders." Two-day workshop presented at the Association for Contextual Behavioural Science Australia and New Zealand Chapter Annual Conference, Sunshine Coast, Australia, 2014.

SOURCES FOR ACTIVITIES

Activity 8: Inviting Your Thoughts and Feelings. Adapted from Coyne, L. W. "Using ACT with Children, Adolescents and Parents: Getting Experiential in Family Work." Conference session presented at the Australian Psychological Society Child, Adolescent, and Family Psychology Interest Group, Adelaide, SA, Australia, 2011.

Activity 15: Singing Your Thoughts. Adapted from Hayes, S. C., and S. Smith. 2005. *Get Out of Your Mind and Into Your Life: The New Acceptance and Commitment Therapy.* Oakland, CA: New Harbinger Publications.

Activity 24: Floppy Octopus. Adapted from Saltzman, A. and P. Goldin. 2008. "Mindfulness-Based Stress Reduction for School-Age Children." In L. A. Greco and S. C. Hayes (Eds.), *Acceptance and Mindfulness Treatments for Children and Adolescents: A Practitioner's Guide* (pp. 139–161). Oakland, CA: New Harbinger Publications.

Activity 25: Staying Here While Eating. Adapted from Saltzman, A., and P. Goldin. 2008. "Mindfulness-Based Stress Reduction for School-Age Children." In L. A. Greco and S. C. Hayes (Eds.), *Acceptance and Mindfulness Treatments for Children and Adolescents: A Practitioner's Guide* (pp. 139–161). Oakland, CA: New Harbinger Publications.

Activity 30: Under the Sea. Adapted from Hayes, S. C., and S. Smith. 2005. *Get Out of Your Mind and Into Your Life: The New Acceptance and Commitment Therapy.* Oakland, CA: New Harbinger Publications.

Activity 33: Still, Quiet Ship. Adapted from Coyne, L. W. 2011. "Using ACT with Children, Adolescents and Parents: Getting Experiential in Family Work." Conference session presented at the Australian Psychological Society Child, Adolescent, and Family Psychology Interest Group, Adelaide, SA, Australia, 2011.

Activity 38: Imagining a Calm and Quiet Place. Adapted from Bluth, K. 2017. *The Self-Compassion Workbook for Teens: Mindfulness and Compassion Skills to Overcome Criticism and Embrace Who You Are.* Oakland, CA: New Harbinger Publications, and Neff, K., and C. Germer. 2018. *The Mindful Self-Compassion Workbook: A Proven Way to Accept Yourself, Build Inner Strength, and Thrive.* New York: Guilford Press.

Activity 39: Thoughts, Feelings, and Actions. Adapted from Kolts, R. L. 2016. *CFT Made Simple: A Clinician's Guide to Practicing Compassion-Based Therapy.* Oakland, CA: New Harbinger Publications.

Tamar D. Black, PhD, is an educational and developmental psychologist in Melbourne, Victoria, Australia. She runs a private practice working with children, adolescents, young adults, and parents. Tamar has extensive experience providing clinical supervision to early career and highly experienced psychologists. She also provides training in acceptance and commitment therapy (ACT) to clinicians and teachers. She is author of the professional guide, *ACT for Treating Children.*

Foreword writer **Russ Harris** is an internationally acclaimed ACT trainer; and author of the best-selling ACT-based self-help book, *The Happiness Trap*, which has sold more than one million copies and been published in thirty languages.

Did you know there are **free tools** you can download for this book?

Free tools are things like **worksheets**, **guided meditation exercises**, and **more** that will help you get the most out of your book.

You can download free tools for this book— whether you bought or borrowed it, in any format, from any source—from the New Harbinger website. All you need is a NewHarbinger.com account. Just use the URL provided in this book to view the free tools that are available for it. Then, click on the "download" button for the free tool you want, and follow the prompts that appear to log in to your NewHarbinger.com account and download the material.

You can also save the free tools for this book to your **Free Tools Library** so you can access them again anytime, just by logging in to your account! Just look for this button on the book's free tools page.

+ Save this to my free tools library

If you need help accessing or downloading free tools, visit **newharbinger.com/faq** or contact us at **customerservice@newharbinger.com**.